Blue Banner Biography

Joe Flacco

Heidi Krumenauer

Mitchell Lane
PUBLISHERS
P.O. Box 196
Hockessin, Delaware 19707
Visit us on the web: www.mitchelllane.com
Comments? email us: mitchelllane@mitchelllane.com

Mitchell Lane
PUBLISHERS

Printing   1   2   3   4   5   6   7   8   9

Blue Banner Biographies

Akon	Alan Jackson	Alicia Keys
Allen Iverson	Ashanti	Ashlee Simpson
Ashton Kutcher	Avril Lavigne	Bernie Mac
Beyoncé	Bow Wow	Brett Favre
Britney Spears	Carrie Underwood	Chris Brown
Chris Daughtry	Christina Aguilera	Christopher Paul Curtis
Ciara	Clay Aiken	Cole Hamels
Condoleezza Rice	Corbin Bleu	Daniel Radcliffe
David Ortiz	Derek Jeter	Eminem
Eve	Fergie (Stacy Ferguson)	50 Cent
Gwen Stefani	Ice Cube	Jamie Foxx
Ja Rule	Jay-Z	Jennifer Lopez
Jessica Simpson	J. K. Rowling	**Joe Flacco**
John Legend	Johnny Depp	JoJo
Justin Berfield	Justin Timberlake	Kanye West
Kate Hudson	Keith Urban	Kelly Clarkson
Kenny Chesney	Kristen Stewart	Lance Armstrong
Leona Lewis	Lil Wayne	Lindsay Lohan
Mariah Carey	Mario	Mary J. Blige
Mary-Kate and Ashley Olsen	Miguel Tejada	Missy Elliott
Nancy Pelosi	Natasha Bedingfield	Nelly
Orlando Bloom	P. Diddy	Paris Hilton
Peyton Manning	Pink	Queen Latifah
Rihanna	Ron Howard	Rudy Giuliani
Sally Field	Sean Kingston	Selena
Shakira	Shontelle Layne	Soulja Boy Tell 'Em
Taylor Swift	T.I.	Timbaland
Tim McGraw	Toby Keith	Usher
Vanessa Anne Hudgens	Zac Efron	

Library of Congress Cataloging-in-Publication Data
Krumenauer, Heidi.
  Joe Flacco / by Heidi Krumenauer.
    p. cm. — (Blue banner biographies)
  Includes bibliographical references and index.
  ISBN 978-1-58415-771-7 (library bound)
  1. Flacco, Joe—Juvenile literature. 2. Football players—United States—Biography—Juvenile literature. 3. Quarterbacks (Football)—United States—Biography—Juvenile literature. I. Title.
  GV939.F555K78 2010
  796.332092—dc22
  [B]
                                                                                        2009006305

ABOUT THE AUTHOR: Heidi Krumenauer is a regular contributor to several print and online publications. Since 2006, she has contributed chapters to 10 nonfiction book projects. Heidi's first book, *Why Does Grandma Have a Wibble?*, was released in 2007. She also wrote *Brett Favre, Rihanna, Jimmie Johnson,* and *Sean Kingston* for Mitchell Lane Publishers. Heidi graduated from the University of Wisconsin–Platteville with a degree in technical communications management. She is in upper management for a Fortune 400 insurance company. Heidi and her husband, Jeff, are raising their two sons, Noah and Payton, in southern Wisconsin.

PUBLISHER'S NOTE: The following story has been thoroughly researched, and to the best of our knowledge represents a true story. While every possible effort has been made to ensure accuracy, the publisher will not assume liability for damages caused by inaccuracies in the data and makes no warranty on the accuracy of the information contained herein. This story has not been authorized or endorsed by Joe Flacco.

Blue Banner Biography

Joe Flacco had an astounding rookie year as quarterback for the NFL's Baltimore Ravens.

Draft Day

*I*t wasn't a typical Saturday afternoon in the Flacco living room. Most days are usually a little less stressful, but on April 26, 2008, the Flacco family—mom, dad, brothers, sister, aunts, uncles, cousins, and grandparents—gathered together for the 2008 NFL Draft. University of Delaware quarterback Joe Flacco was a potential pick, and this was the day he would find out if he would be called to play professional football.

"My mom has six brothers, and I have five siblings. There are a lot of people here," said Joe, talking about the crowd gathered at his home, hoping to see him get a shot at the NFL. "Believe me, my house isn't big enough to hold everybody, but everybody's just having a blast, and everybody's just as excited as I am." His mother, Karen, said, "It's not often that you get to see your child's dream come true right in front of your eyes."

Draft day normally comes with some analysis by the television sports commentators, but Karen was not worried about what they might say about her son. "Most people really don't have many bad things to say. They picked on his footwork, but I think they were grasping at straws or something," she said.

Baltimore Ravens offensive coordinator Cam Cameron wasn't picking on Joe. In fact, Cameron was looking for what he called a "quick-twitch guy," and he knew Joe Flacco fit the bill. "He's quick with his arm, and he's quick for a tall guy," he says. "I think that's a little uncommon. In our system, we'd like our quarterback to have nimble feet, have an explosive arm, be quick with the football, and I actually think Joe has that."

> "We'd like our quarterback to have nimble feet, have an explosive arm, be quick with the football, and I actually think Joe has that," says Cameron.

The Ravens felt that Joe was the complete package they needed to lead their team. "He has a rocket arm, he's smart, he's a big kid, he's played in bad weather, which we like," director of college scouting Eric DeCosta noted on the Ravens web site. "Joe was the guy that separated himself from the other guys."

At approximately 5:00 P.M. on April 26, Ravens general manager Ozzie Newsome made a phone call that would forever change Joe's life. The Ravens made some trades before choosing Joe as a first-round draft pick. Newsome offered Joe the opportunity to become the eighteenth overall selection in the NFL Draft. The best thing for Joe was that he would be able to play professional football in a stadium only 105 miles from his small hometown of Audubon, New Jersey. His family, die-hard Philadelphia Eagles fans, would also have to adjust to cheering for new colors.

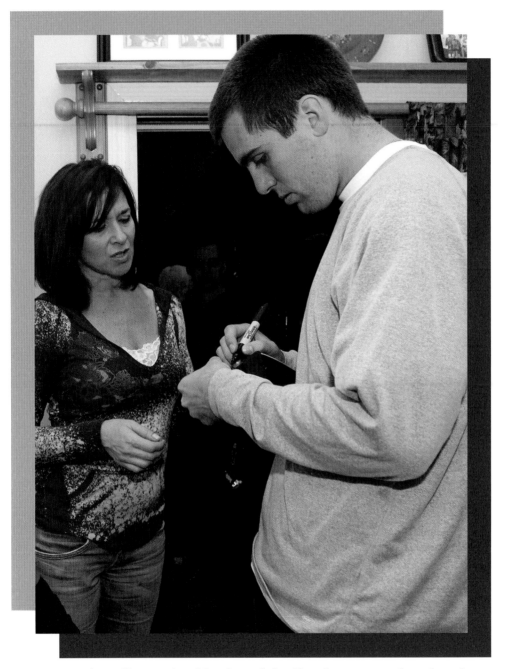

As soon as the call came in, friends and family who were gathered at the Flacco house began asking Joe for his autograph.

At Joe's first press conference as a Baltimore Raven, general manager
Ozzie Newsome presented Joe with a jersey. He was the team's first-round
draft pick, and during the year Joe really proved that he was "Number 1"
in the 2008 season.

Joe talked about his excitement in his first press conference the day after the Ravens drafted him. He told reporters, "It was really exciting for me yesterday to have Ozzie call me and tell me they were actually trading up to pick me. So to actually have that happen, it was just a big deal for me. I was walking around my house all nervous about missing a phone call and all of a sudden my phone was ringing and it was Ozzie Newsome. I knew it was a Baltimore area code, but I didn't know why they were calling me yet. They had eight more picks to go. For them to tell me they were going to pick me, that was really exciting. I'm ready to get down here and work really hard to prove to everybody that they made a good decision picking me."

> *"I'm ready to get down here and work really hard to prove to everybody that they made a good decision picking me."*

Joe signed a five-year, thirty-million-dollar contract with the Baltimore Ravens on July 18, 2008. Would he have to make a few adjustments to playing in the NFL? Absolutely! Jumping to the NFL from the University of Delaware — where he played against teams like Towson and Monmouth, in front of crowds that averaged 18,000 — would be a change, but Joe was confident. In a press conference in April 2008, he said, "I'm just as prepared as anybody else."

Standing six-foot-six, 230 pounds, with a strong throwing arm, Joe Flacco is a dominant figure on the football field and a threat to his opponents. Known to the media as Joe Cool, Joe prefers the nickname "Bazooka Joe, like the gum."

Small-town Kid with a Big-time Arm

Joseph Vincent Flacco (FLAAK-oh) was born on January 16, 1985, to Stephen and Karen Flacco. Joe grew up in Audubon, New Jersey, outside of Philadelphia. He has four younger brothers and one younger sister. Joe comes from a family of athletes, including his parents. Steve played football and baseball at the University of Pennsylvania. He dreamed of playing professional baseball, but instead went to work in the mortgage business. Karen also had a love of sports, and was a standout in both basketball and softball at Trenton State (now the College of New Jersey).

With parents who loved sports, it wasn't a surprise that Joe had a batting cage in the backyard. Steve tutored his son in football, but he was never his coach. Even so, Joe said his dad was always honest, telling him when he was playing well and when he was terrible.

At a young age, Joe found he had a natural ability to throw the ball. He started playing organized football in seventh grade, but he wasn't always the quarterback. He played other positions also.

Joe's family is supportive of his professional football career. Pictured with Joe on draft day in Audubon, New Jersey, are his four younger brothers, Brian, Mike, Tom, and John; his younger sister, Stephanie; and his parents, Karen and Steve.

    Growing up, Joe always dreamed of playing in the NFL someday. Other dreams were a little more unrealistic. Once Joe told his father that he wanted to look just like Michael Jordan. When Joe played games of pickup football with his friends, he loved to pretend he was one of the football greats like Barry Sanders, Jerry Rice, or Joe Montana.

    Joe attended Audubon High School in New Jersey and had only 167 kids in his graduating class. It's also the place where his football career began. He was a three-year starter, throwing for 5,137 career yards. He was recognized several times for his accomplishments at Audubon High, including being named twice to the All–South Jersey team, twice to the first team All–Colonial Conference, and twice to the New Jersey All–Group II.

Joe excelled at more than football, earning three letters in baseball and two in basketball. Academically, he was at the head of his class, attaining the Principal's Honor Roll.

Joe wasn't at the head of the class in just schoolwork, however. He might have been at the *top* of his class — in height! Joe's growth spurt started early — in eighth and ninth grades. A growth chart marked in pencil on the doorway in the Flacco family's living room shows that Joe was five-foot-eleven in eighth grade. That was taller than his father! At the start of high school, Joe measured six-foot-two. His final measurement is scratched into the doorway at six-foot-six. Joe's family has benefited from his tallness. "I'm pretty big for my family, so people tend to use me to reach the things up high," Joe said on the Baltimore Ravens web site. "My grandmom always jokes with me around Christmas time about putting stuff on top of the tree."

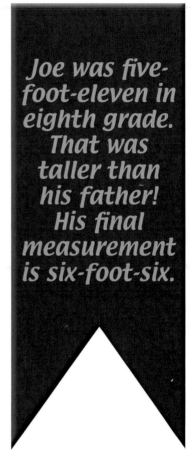

Joe was five-foot-eleven in eighth grade. That was taller than his father! His final measurement is six-foot-six.

As quarterback for the University of Delaware Blue Hens, Joe wore the same number as he does for the Ravens—lucky #5.

Blue Hen Days

*P*laying college football became a common discussion at the Flacco home when coaches began recruiting Joe at the beginning of his junior year of high school. Even so, Joe knew that he needed to be serious about his college major. In a question-and-answer session on the Baltimore Ravens web site, Joe said, "I went into the business school right away, and I made up my mind two years in that that was it. I was an accounting major. I like math."

Joe turned down an offer from the University of Delaware in high school. He also turned down a scholarship to Rutgers University. Instead he accepted a scholarship from the University of Pittsburgh and enrolled there in 2003. He was red-shirted the first season, which means although he was part of the team, he did not play in any games. In 2004, he was the backup to starter Tyler Palko and played only briefly in three games. Joe was discouraged by the lack of playing time, so he decided to transfer to the University of Delaware in 2005. He joined the team in August, but he was ineligible to play because he had not been released from his scholarship at Pittsburgh. Under the athletic rules, he

During a playoff game on December 8, 2007, Joe threw for 243 yards and two touchdowns, helping his number thirteen Delaware Blue Hens defeat fourth-ranked Southern Illinois 20-17. The Blue Hens advanced to the Football Championship Subdivision title game.

wouldn't be eligible to play until 2006. Even though he didn't see any action on the field during his first year in Delaware, he participated in practice drills with the team.

Joe finally got some playing time for the Delaware Blue Hens in 2006. He earned a starting spot as quarterback after a preseason competition with senior Ryan Carty, and started all 11 games. Joe led the Blue Hens to one of their best seasons for passing offense. In his first season, he averaged 253 passing yards per game—ranking him ninth in the NCAA. It was also the third highest average in Delaware's history. He averaged 26.3 points per game—ranking him fourth in the A-10 Conference. Joe averaged 356.6 total yards per game—30th in the NCAA. In that same season, he passed for 2,783 yards and 18 touchdowns. He earned the Blue Hen Touchdown Club Offensive Player of the Week three times.

Even with records and awards, Joe didn't see his future as clearly as others. During his junior season at Delaware, he asked his coach's permission to join the baseball team in the spring. According to the *New York Times*, Coach K.C. Keeler responded: "Baseball? You realize you're going to be a draft choice next year?" A surprised Joe said, "Really?"

During his senior year in 2007, Joe continued to lead the Blue Hens, completing 331 passes for 4,263 yards and 23 touchdowns. He ranked sixth in the nation with an average of 460.6 yards per game in total offense. Joe earned the All-American, All-East, All–Eastern College Athletic Conference, and All–Colonial Athletic Association honors as a senior. He was also the ECAC Player of the Year and CAA Co-Offensive Player of the Year. He helped lead the Blue Hens to the NCAA Division I Football Championship Subdivision national title game, where they lost to Appalachian State 49-21.

Coach K.C. Keeler responded, ". . . You realize you're going to be a draft choice next year?" A surprised Joe said, "Really?"

Overall, Joe started in 26 games for Delaware. He holds the school record for pass completions, having made 595 of 938 attempts. He threw for 41 touchdowns, had 15 interceptions, and was sacked 48 times. He rushed 147 times for 76 yards.

Joe's rise to fame didn't happen on prominent college football fields such as USC, Alabama, or Notre Dame, but he

Joe and general manager Ozzie Newsome share a laugh during a news conference on July 21, 2008, in Westminster, Maryland. Joe signed his contract that day and reported to coach John Harbaugh's first training camp.

was consistent and unshakable — traits that are highly desirable in the NFL. Joe's style was turning heads — especially those in Baltimore.

Rookie QB Makes History

Upon learning that he would be playing with the Baltimore Ravens, first-round draft pick Joe Flacco was eager to start playing with his new team. "I want to get out there on the field and prove that I can," he told reporters in a press conference the day after he was drafted. "It's going to be up to the coaches to make that final decision, but it's going to be up to me to prove that I'm ready." But was he ready to be the *starting* quarterback? Joe said yes.

The Ravens' coaching staff had something different in mind.

General manager Ozzie Newsome had intended for Joe to sit on the sidelines during his rookie year in the NFL. He thought it would be best for Joe to get a little more experience watching from the bench. However, medical issues with the Ravens' other quarterbacks made it impossible for Newsome to stick to that plan. QB Kyle Boller suffered a season-ending shoulder injury in a preseason game. Former Heisman Trophy winner Troy Smith was in line to take Boller's place for the first game of the season, but he came down with a rare tonsil infection. As the third-string quarterback, Joe was

On September 7, 2008, Joe charged the field with teammates Todd Bauman and Le'Ron McClain for the season opener against the Cincinnati Bengals — and to be the starting quarterback in his first game in the NFL.

asked to step in and take control of the Ravens for the season opener against the Cincinnati Bengals.

In Joe's first game, he completed 15 of 29 passes for 129 yards. He didn't throw for a touchdown, but he did cross the goal line! In his first NFL start, Joe set a team record with a 38-yard rushing touchdown—the longest rushing touchdown by a quarterback in Ravens franchise history. The Ravens won the game 17-10.

Joe's performance and winning streak didn't stop there. In week 7, he enjoyed his first career road victory against the

Miami Dolphins. During that game, Joe had his best career performance, throwing for more than 230 yards and maintaining a 64.2 completion percentage.

In week 13, Joe topped his personal best, throwing for 280 yards and two touchdowns. In the previous seven games, Joe had risen to the top of the NFL with a passer rating of 99.1 — the best of any quarterback in that time period.

In week 16, Joe led the Ravens to victory over the Dallas Cowboys in the last game to be played at Texas Stadium. He was the first rookie quarterback to win at Texas Stadium since the Pittsburgh Steelers' Ben Roethlisberger in 2004.

And then Joe topped himself again! In week 17, he passed for 297 yards. He completed 17 of 23 passes for a QB rating of 115.8 in the 27-7 win over the Jacksonville Jaguars.

Over the course of the regular season, Joe had been named AFC Offensive Player of the Week, NFL Rookie of the Week, NFL Players Association Rookie of the Week, and NFL Rookie of the Month.

> *Joe's rookie season was anything but usual—mostly because it didn't end with the regular season.*

Joe's rookie season was anything but usual — mostly because it didn't end with the regular season. The Ravens had earned a wild-card spot in the 2008 NFL play-offs. Joe became only the third rookie quarterback in NFL history to win his first postseason start, and he was the first rookie to do it on the road. Joe led the Ravens to a 27-9 win over the Miami Dolphins. During that game, he ran the ball into the end zone for the game's final touchdown.

Joe had Pittsburgh Steelers Troy Polamalu in his sights, but it wasn't enough to score a win during a regular season game. One month later, the Ravens and the Steelers met again on the field, both vying for a trip to the Super Bowl.

On January 29, 2009, Joe was named the Diet Pepsi NFL Rookie of the Year. More than one million fans submitted votes to select the winner from five finalists, who were chosen for their outstanding performances during the 2008 season.

One week later, Joe was celebrating another win, this one over the Tennessee Titans — a win that would put his name in the NFL record books. No other rookie quarterback had won two play-off games.

On January 18, 2009, the Baltimore Ravens faced the Pittsburgh Steelers in the AFC Championship Game. Joe played a tough game, but his statistics weren't as impressive as they had been during the previous weeks. He completed just 13 of 30 passes for 141 yards, was sacked three times, and threw three interceptions. Just one win shy of the national championship game, twenty-four-year-old Joe's dreams of being the first rookie QB in the Super Bowl were shattered when the Steelers defeated the Ravens 23-14.

CHAPTER
5

"Joe Cool"

Joe Flacco never had a job working at a gas station or waiting tables at the local diner. His first job was with the NFL as a starting quarterback. That job doesn't come with a minimum-wage salary. In fact, his annual salary as a rookie was $295,000, with the opportunity to increase that amount depending on playing time and bonuses for play-off games. He also had a five-year, thirty-million-dollar contract.

So, how do professional football players spend that kind of money? Most of them might splurge a little on fancy cars or motorcycles. Joe bought a lawn mower for his mother instead. No kidding! Joe doesn't even own a car. In fact, he's never owned a car. He showed up at training camp driving his grandmother's 1990 Volvo. Shortly after that, he was driving a BMW loaner from a local car dealership with a sticker in the back window that read: "This is a courtesy car." Joe also wasn't too proud to accept rides from his parents: They dropped him off at the stadium for his first game.

What about his house? Certainly, Joe bought a mansion with the money, didn't he? Although he has enough money to buy a house on the beach, another one in the mountains, and probably a few others, Joe lives a simple life in a two-bedroom apartment with his younger brother Mike. When Joe was asked in a press conference if he had made any big purchases, he said, "I've got more things to worry about than going out and buying stuff."

According to the *Baltimore Sun*, a college friend and teammate said of Joe, "He's in a glamorous position, but it doesn't go to his head. He's a starting quarterback in the

During a game against the New York Giants on November 16, 2008, Joe's Ravens suffered a loss of 30-10. Joe outpassed Giants QB Eli Manning by 11 yards.

NFL, but he's the same person that he's always been. That's what separates him from other people."

While many star quarterbacks are making headlines by dating celebrities, Joe happily keeps his personal life a little more low-key, taking his offensive linemen out for dinner on Friday nights. On most evenings, though, you might find Joe on his couch in front of the television. Joe's father, Steve, describes his son's life as "boring," but he knows that in order for Joe to do well on the field, he needs to put in some extra time watching game films.

> "I definitely am a low-key guy. I'm not a rah-rah guy. I really just want to prove to them that I can play football."

Teammates and Ravens head coach John Harbaugh describe Joe as grounded and laid-back, leaving people to wonder if he ever gets upset. When speaking to the media, Joe shows little emotion, often talking without much excitement in his voice. "That's just Joe," says Coach Harbaugh. And Joe agrees. "I definitely am a low-key guy," he said in an interview with the *Baltimore Examiner*. "I'm not a rah-rah guy. I really just want to prove to them that I can play football."

"Joe is just a very confident person, but he's not comfortable being a rock star," Coach Keeler told the [Wilmington, Delaware] *Examiner* in 2008. Joe might not be a rock star, but he does realize the importance of giving back to the community. Like his peers, Joe donates time to charity organizations. During his first year with the Ravens, Joe was involved with the Baltimore chapter of Special Olympics. Raising money sometimes means taking a bit of a risk — or

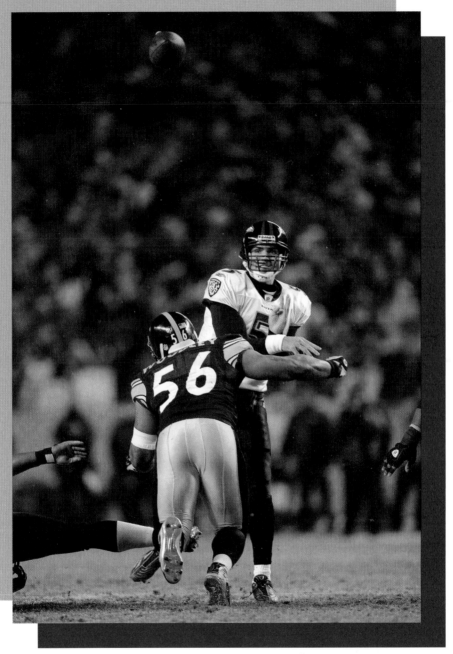

Joe holds off linebacker LaMarr Woodley of the Pittsburgh Steelers in the AFC Championship game. Unfortunately the Ravens lost, and Joe was forced to watch the Super Bowl from home.

in Joe's case, a plunge. Joe joined 11,000 others in a Polar Bear Plunge, where he jumped into the icy waters of the Chesapeake Bay to help raise $2 million for charity.

While he was quickly given the nickname "Joe Cool" by his fans and the media, Joe's family has a different impression. "They tell me how dorky I look on TV," Joe wrote in his profile on the Ravens web site. And according to his brother Thomas, it's weird having a brother in the NFL. Why? "Because I can pick him on my team when I play Madden Football," he told the *Star-Ledger* in November 2008. "He's my brother and he's on a video game. I kind of have to pick him because he's my brother, but in the video game, he's not very good."

Joe's brother John looks at it this way: "The way he's been playing, and all the stuff that's surrounding him is pretty cool."

With any luck, the new cool life that Joe is living might extend to another family member. Younger brother Mike has been turning heads on the baseball field, and the family hopes that he will be drafted by a Major League team. If that happens, Joe will, no doubt, lend some brotherly advice about what it takes to succeed on the field — because he's proven there's more to success than a powerful arm.

Year	Team	G	GS	Comp	Att	Pct	Yards	YPA	Lg	TD	Int	Rate
2008	BAL	9	7	257	428	60	2,971	6.94	70	14	12	80.3
Total		9	7	257	428	60	2971	6.94	70	14	12	80.3

(G=Games, GS=Games started, Comp=Completions, Att=Attempts, Pct=Percentage, YPA=Yards per attempt, Lg=Longest pass, TD=Touchdown, Int=Interceptions, Rate=Quarterback rating)

CHRONOLOGY

1985   Joseph Vincent Flacco is born on January 16.

2003   Joe graduates from Audubon High School in Audubon, New Jersey. He enrolls at the University of Pittsburgh in the fall.

2005   Joe transfers to the University of Delaware.

2006   Joe is the starting quarterback for the University of Delaware, playing all 11 games.

2007   As a senior, Joe earns All-American, All-East, All-ECAC, and All-CAA honors.

2008   Joe is drafted by the Baltimore Ravens on April 26, signing a five-year, thirty-million-dollar contract. He begins his NFL career as a starting QB on week 1 of the regular season. Joe also signs a three-year contract with Reebok.

2009   Joe is the first rookie QB to play in the third round of the NFL play-offs. Joe leads the Ravens to the AFC Championship Game, but they are defeated by the Pittsburgh Steelers on January 18. He wins the NFL Diet Pepsi Rookie of the Year Award.

Books

Crompton, Samuel Willard. *Peyton Manning*. New York: Checkmark Books, 2008.

Krumenauer, Heidi. *Brett Favre*. Hockessin, DE: Mitchell Lane Publishers, 2008.

Sandler, Michael. *Ben Roethlisberger*. New York: Bearport Publishing, 2009.

Works Consulted

Baltimore Ravens: *News*, "Joe Flacco Bio"
http://www.baltimoreravens.com/News/Articles/2008/04/Joe_Flacco_Bio.aspx

Baltimore Ravens: *News*, "Outtakes: Joe Flacco"
http://www.baltimoreravens.com/News/Articles/2008/11/Outtakes_-_Joe_Flacco.aspx

Battista, Judy. "Measuring Up, on the Doorway and on the Draft Board." *The New York Times*. April 24, 2008.
http://www.nytimes.com/2008/04/24/sports/football/24flacco.html?scp=2&sq=judy+battista&st=nyt

Cooney, Bob. "Flacco Household Has Rooting Interest in Joe, Ravens." *Philadelphia Daily News*. October 2, 2008.
http://www.philly.com/dailynews/columnists/bob_cooney/30082239.html

———. "Ravens QB Flacco Not Playing Like a Rookie." *Philadelphia Daily News*. November 18, 2008.
http://www.philly.com/dailynews/sports/20081118_Ravens_QB_Flacco_not_playing_like_a_rookie.html

Duffy, Mike. "Draft Profile: Flacco Moves to the Bigs"
http://www.baltimoreravens.com/News/Articles/2008/04/Draft_Profile_-_Flacco_Moves_to_the_Bigs.aspx

Hagen, Paul. "Flacco a Leading Factor in Ravens' Success." *Philadelphia Daily News*. January 15, 2009.
http://www.philly.com/philly/sports/eagles/20090115_Flacco_a_leading_factor_in_Ravens__success.html

FURTHER READING

Hensley, Jamison. " 'It's Just Football,' Says Ravens' Joe Cool."
The Baltimore Sun. January 4, 2009.
http://www.baltimoresun.com/sports/football/balte.sp.
flacco04jan04,0,198011.story

Manahan, Kevin. "Audubon's Flacco Learns Giant Lesson in
Ravens' Loss." *The Star-Ledger.* November 16, 2008.
http://www.nj.com/giants/index.ssf/2008/11/
audubons_flacco_learns_giant_l.html

NFL.com: NFL Draft 2008, "Prospects: Joe Flacco"
http://www.nfl.com/draft/profiles/joe-flacco?id=382

Powell, Camille. "Flacco Hopes Adjustment to NFL Is Not a Tall
Tale." *The Washington Post.* April 28, 2008.
http://www.washingtonpost.com/wp-dyn/content/
story/2008/04/27/ST2008042702164.html

Snyder, Ron. "Flacco: From Blue Hen to Raven." *The Examiner.*
May 6, 2008.
http://www.examiner.com/a-1376719~Flacco__From_Blue_
Hen_to_Raven.html

Transcript of Baltimore Ravens Press Conference. April 27, 2008.

Transcript of Baltimore Ravens Press Conference. July 21, 2008.

University of Delaware Athletics: *Roster—Football,* "Joe Flacco"
http://www.bluehens.com/sportsinfo/football/
roster05-flacco.html

Web Addresses
Baltimore Ravens
    http://www.baltimoreravens.com
National Football League
    http://www.nfl.com
University of Delaware Athletics
    http://www.bluehens.com

INDEX